WELCOME TO THE WORLD OF

Coyotes

Diane Swanson

Whitecap Books
Vancouver / Toronto

Edited by Elizabeth McLean
Cover design by Steve Penner
Interior design by Margaret Ng
Typeset by Maxine Lea
Photo research by Tanya Lloyd
Cover photograph by Thomas Kitchin/firstlight.ca
Photo credits: Michael Quinton/firstlight.ca iv, 10, 14; Thomas Kitchin/firstlight.ca 2, 12; Mary Clay/Dembinsky Photo Assoc 4; Jim Battles/Dembinsky Photo Assoc 6; Darrell Gulin/Dembinsky Photo Assoc 8; Mark Degner 16; Tim Christie/timchristie.com 18; Victoria Hurst/firstlight.ca 20; Wayne Lynch 22, 24, 26

Printed and bound in Canada

National Library of Canada Cataloguing in Publication Data

Swanson, Diane, 1944–
    Welcome to the world of coyotes

    Includes index.
    ISBN 1-55285-308-X

    1. Coyotes—Juvenile literature. I. Title.
QL737.C22S898 2001   j599.77'25   C2001-910984-9

For more information on this series and other Whitecap Books titles, visit our web site at www.whitecap.ca

The publisher acknowledges the support of the Canada Council for the Arts and the Cultural Services Branch of the Government of British Columbia for our publishing program. We acknowledge the financial support of the Government of Canada through the Book Publishing Industry Development Program for our publishing activities.

Contents

World of Difference

PRAIRIE WOLF, BRUSH WOLF, LITTLE WOLF—all names people call the coyote. It's a wild dog with a bushy tail and a pointed face, but the coyote is no wolf.

Bigger than a fox and much smaller than a wolf, a good-sized coyote weighs about as much as a little dalmatian dog. Males are usually larger than females, and coyotes that live in cities—where there's plenty of food—grow heavier than those in the country.

The color of their coats varies with the coyote. The fur is often a mixture of gray, tan, and white, but it can also include black. Some coyotes have coats that are mostly

Even in winter, a coyote can sniff out whatever is around.

1

With its eyes focused on a mouse, a coyote leaps after it.

reddish or yellow-brown. During winter, they are normally lighter in color.

It's lucky that the coyote has keen senses. They help it find food and escape enemies. A coyote's eyes can spot small movements among the trees or in long grass. Its ears can hear the rustling of tiny feet beneath blankets of snow. And its nose can sniff a hiding rabbit—or an approaching mountain lion.

To chase down food or outrun danger, the coyote depends on a body built for speed. Its long legs are well designed for racing, and its tail provides balance. Held out to one side, it helps the coyote make sudden sharp turns while running. No wonder coyotes can survive 8 years. Some live to be 10 or more.

Coyotes often amaze people. Here are just some of the reasons why:

- In short bursts, coyotes can reach speeds of 65 kilometres (40 miles) an hour.
- City coyotes sometimes learn to follow dairy delivery trucks and drink milk left at doorways.
- During dry summer months, thirsty coyotes may dig to find underground water.

Where in the World

COYOTES ARE CRITTERS OF NORTH AND CENTRAL AMERICA—and nowhere else on Earth. At one time, they lived only in western parts of the continent, usually in woods and open country such as grasslands. But as people cleared dense forests for towns and farms, they created more space for coyotes—and more food, too.

Settlers also drove back two of the coyote's main enemies: mountain lions and wolves. That made it easier for coyotes to grow in numbers and spread out.

Today there are many more coyotes than there once were, and they live

The dry rocky lands of Arizona are home to some coyotes.

5

A coyote in a parking lot is no surprise in many cities.

throughout much of North and Central America. They have even moved into huge cities. You might spot them in golf courses, cemeteries, and parks. They travel within cities by running along beaches, alleys, and railway tracks. And they can climb fences— or burrow beneath them—to get into backyards and gardens.

The space a coyote needs depends on the size of its family and the amount of food available. All that changes from season to season, year to year, and place to place.

Before female coyotes give birth, they snuggle into dens. But most of the time, coyotes just rest on the ground. They form beds by turning round and round, packing down the grass or snow. Many pet dogs—coyote cousins—do the same thing, even inside houses where there's nothing to pack down.

FOLLOWING THEIR NOSES

Smells of food—including garbage and dead animals —attract coyotes. It was probably the odor of rotting seals that first lured coyotes from Nova Scotia to the island of Newfoundland in the 1980s. As they walked across the ice-covered water, they fed on the dead seals.

About 100 years earlier, coyotes followed their noses northward. They ate garbage and dead mules left by gold miners heading for Alaska and Yukon.

7

World Full of Food

YOU CAN'T CALL COYOTES FUSSY EATERS. They feed on almost everything: grass, nuts, fruits, veggies, eggs, insects, snakes, skunks, bats, birds, fish, and frogs. But mostly they eat rabbits, hares, and rodents such as mice and squirrels. Having a huge menu makes it possible for coyotes to live just about anywhere.

A coyote finds its meals quite easily—even underwater. It sticks its head into streams to grab fish and dives for crayfish.

Although a coyote can chase a fast-hopping rabbit or hare, it prefers not to waste energy. Belly to the ground, the

If there's food in the river, a coyote plunges right in.

9

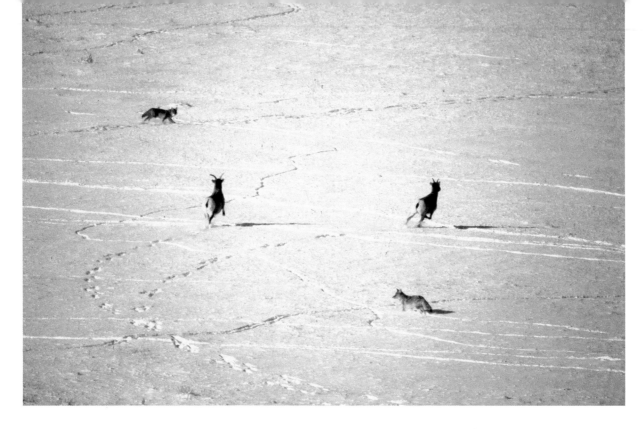

Two coyotes team up to hunt bighorn sheep.

coyote often sneaks up close, then pounces on its prey.

Sometimes a coyote plays tricks to grab lunch. It might pretend to be dead until a crow comes close, then snatch the bird. Or the coyote might trail a badger to a den of ground squirrels and wait while the badger digs into the den. When the squirrels try to escape, the coyote can grab one.

Coyotes also work in pairs to nab a meal. One coyote might scare a hare toward the waiting jaws of its partner. Or it might jump around to get the hare's attention while the partner sneaks up from behind.

When coyotes hunt a bigger animal, such as a deer, they work together as a team. They may take turns chasing it, so they can stay fresh while the deer wears out. When it drops down exhausted, the team moves in.

THREE CHEEPS FOR COYOTES!

Birds should be cheering—or cheeping—for coyotes. They sometimes feed on birds, but they scare off or eat many of the other animals that hunt for birds.

Around San Diego, California, scientists found that coyotes increased the number of birds by reducing the number of opossums, foxes, raccoons, and pet cats. The cats, alone, had been killing more than 15 birds each every year. People who keep their pets indoors save birds from cats—and cats from coyotes.

11

World of Words

Nose to the sky, a coyote howls to its partner.

EXPECT RAIN WHEN COYOTES WAIL—or so Mexican folklore claims. Coyotes can't predict weather, but they do have plenty to say. Their barks, growls, yips, yelps, and howls are loaded with meaning. Parent coyotes, for instance, use sounds to call their young pups for dinner and warn them to run or hide from danger. Pups talk to their parents to report hunger, pain, and fear.

Growling or huffing is how coyotes usually threaten something—or someone—that's close by. Barks or bark-howls make threats from a distance: "Go away!"

13

Not surprisingly, words of welcome sound much different. "Woo-oo-wow," says a coyote when it greets another. Or it might make a low-pitched whine, meaning the same thing. If the approaching coyote is more powerful, the greeter whines in a high-pitched voice instead. It also holds its tail low as it wags.

In body language— narrowed eyes and wrinkled snout—a coyote says, "Scat!"

Bark, bark, bark, h-o-w-l! A lone coyote may call out, trying to contact others. Families seem to know if the message comes from one of their members or not. The coyotes answer by howling right back, which can help them get together again.

Sometimes howling seems to produce more howling. Coyotes not only answer calls from other coyotes, but they also respond to the howls of pet dogs and wolves—even to the wails of fire truck and ambulance sirens!

PECOS BILL

Nothing howls like a coyote, except Pecos Bill. At least, that's how the story goes. People still tell tall tales of a young pioneer boy who fell from a covered wagon near the Pecos River in Texas. He was rescued and raised by coyotes.

Pecos Bill learned to run, hunt—even talk—like coyotes. At nighttime, he would join the others to bark, yip, and H-O-W-L at the moon. Some folks say Bill howled so long and so loud he sounded like a hundred coyotes.

New World

COYOTE BIRTHDAYS FALL IN SPRING-TIME. But before the pups arrive, their parents search for nurseries—dens that are dry, hidden, and close to food and water.

Parent coyotes sometimes choose a cave or hollow log as a nursery. They might dig a burrow in a hillside or riverbank. More often, though, they take over an empty den that once belonged to a badger, skunk, or fox. The coyotes clean out the burrow. They might enlarge it and add an extra entrance, too.

Some female coyotes line their nurseries with layers of soft grass, leaves, or fur

A female coyote digs a den for a nursery.

17

Two wee pups
take a peek at
their new world.

pulled from their bellies. Others don't bother providing any lining at all.

A newborn coyote is usually born along with 3 to 5 brothers and sisters. Some pups arrive with as many as 18 others! Their birth size depends a lot on their numbers, but a new coyote weighs only about as much as a large potato.

The pups don't have much hair, and their eyes are shut. They cuddle close to their mother for warmth and safety. For at least a week, she seldom leaves them. Her mate brings her food and guards the den. Others in the family help, too, babysitting when the mother later heads off to hunt for food.

Father coyotes and baby-sitters also help the mother move her pups when she must. For instance, she may change nurseries several times to avoid pests such as fleas.

Inside an old skunk den, things smelled...well...a bit skunky. But that didn't bother the coyote pups piled on top of one another. They had never been outside the den—never sniffed the fresh spring air.

All that was about to change, however. The pups were 10 days old, and their eyelids were starting to flicker. Any minute, they would be able to see. Soon they would crawl to the den's entrance and—blink! sniff!—check out their world.

Small World

LITTLE COYOTES HAVE BIG APPETITES. When they're only about two weeks old, they demand more than milk for dinner. They nibble around the lips of their parents to say, "Share your meals." The grown coyotes throw up some of the food that's in their stomachs. For the pups, vomit is a perfect meal—soft, warm, and nutritious.

As the pups grow, their parents start feeding them whole foods. They begin with small animals, such as insects and mice, and gradually add bigger animals. Later, dinners might include a ground squirrel, then a rabbit.

A coyote starts howling when it's just a young pup.

21

This parent coyote would rather find food for its pup than play.

At first, the parents present the pups with dead animals. Soon they start bringing home live ones for the pups to help kill.

By the time coyote pups are eight or nine weeks old, they're ready to go hunting with their parents. There is still a lot to learn. The pups must practice spotting, stalking, and nabbing animals such as grasshoppers. They inspect the sky for ravens and vultures that have found food the pups might share.

Young coyotes try to avoid becoming meals themselves. They watch out for bobcats, eagles, wolverines, and other enemies. They also obey the sounds their parents use to warn, "Keep still. Be quiet."

After several more months, some of the pups may head out to find their own homes. Others stay with their parents, helping to care for next spring's pups.

HIGH-RISE COYOTE

Searching for food, a young coyote wandered through a passageway linking a river-bank with a tall building in Edmonton, Alberta. Cleaning staff spotted the coyote with its head stuck between the bars of a fifth-floor railing. It managed to squeeze its body through, but fell to a balcony below. There it got its head stuck in another railing.

Police and wildlife officers worked to free the frightened coyote. Then they moved it outside the city.

Fun World

COYOTE PUPS ARE WILDLY PLAYFUL. They run. They leap. They twist and roll. It's not only great fun, it's good exercise, too. All these workouts help the pups grow well and develop strong muscles. And playing wears the pups out, which helps them sleep well.

Coyotes also play with toys. They sneak up on things such as stones, leaves, twigs, cones, bones, and feathers. They grab them and toss or bat them around. Pups even play with their food, flinging it up in the air before gulping it down.

Like people, coyotes sometimes play

"Hey, let's play," a pup signals to its brother.

25

Chomp! One pup grabs another's snout—but it's all in fun.

with others. They pretend to chase, wrestle, hunt—even kill—one another. It's part of the training they need for their later lives as grown coyotes. Playful pups exchange roles, switching back and forth from being "victims" to being "attackers." Parent coyotes sense that the pups are just playing and don't jump in to protect them.

Some coyote games seem like tests of strength. For instance, two pups might tug on the same stick or bone until one of them pulls it away. The winner—the stronger pup— may be the first to get fed by its parents.

When a pup is looking for a playmate, it often sends out signals. It squirms and rolls around on the ground. If no coyote responds, the pup might run around in circles, chasing its own tail.

You have your toys, and coyotes have theirs. But in cities, they play with people's things, too. Young coyotes like to chase tennis balls and golf balls. They pounce on them and chew them up.

Even fuzzy slippers, leather sandals, and rubber tire scraps can become toys for coyotes. Two pups might grab the same one and p-u-l-l, starting a game of tug-of-war. An old rag yanked from a garbage can works just as well.

Index

Collect all Welcome to the World titles

- [ ] **1** Welcome to the World of Wolves
- [ ] **2** Welcome to the World of Whales
- [ ] **3** Welcome to the World of Bears
- [ ] **4** Welcome to the World of Otters
- [ ] **5** Welcome to the World of Owls
- [ ] **6** Welcome to the World of Wild Cats
- [ ] **7** Welcome to the World of Eagles
- [ ] **8** Welcome to the World of Foxes
- [ ] **9** Welcome to the World of Bats
- [ ] **10** Welcome to the World of Raccoons
- [ ] **11** Welcome to the World of Beavers
- [ ] **12** Welcome to the World of Moose
- [ ] **13** Welcome to the World of Skunks
- [ ] **14** Welcome to the World of Porcupines
- [ ] **15** Welcome to the World of Octopuses
- [ ] **16** Welcome to the World of Rabbits and Hares
- [ ] **17** Welcome to the World of Sharks
- [ ] **18** Welcome to the World of Snakes
- [ ] **19** Welcome to the World of Squirrels
- [ ] **20** Welcome to the World of Coyotes